Is Social Security Broke?

Is Social Security Broke?

A Cartoon Guide to the Issues

Text by Barbara R. Bergmann
Illustrations by Jim Bush

Ann Arbor
THE UNIVERSITY OF MICHIGAN PRESS

Published in the United States of America by
The University of Michigan Press
Manufactured in the United States of America
♾Printed on acid-free paper

2003 2002 2001 2000 4 3 2 1

A CIP catalog record for this book is available from the British Library.

Library of Congress Cataloging-in-Publication Data applied for

ISBN 0-472-09743-1 (cloth : alk. paper)
ISBN 0-472-06734-5 (pbk.: alk. paper)

ISBN13 978-0-472-09743-2 (cloth)
ISBN13 978-0-472-06743-5 (paper)
ISBN13 978-0-472-02305-9 (electronic)

Table of Contents

ACKNOWLEDGMENTS

We are grateful to Charlotte Phelps for introducing the two collaborators. We owe thanks to Michael Ames, whose enthusiasm for this project in its early stages gave us the encouragement that helped us to push ahead. Helpful comments were received from Henry Aaron, Peter Diamond, Estelle James, Ralph Estes, Eileen Applebaum, Edie Rasell, Joyce Miller, Phillip Corfman, Harriet Presser, Beverly Cohen, Stuart Cohen, Bette Anne Osterhoudt, Frank Osterhoudt, Alan Isaac, Christopher Clague, Lynn Penner, Suzanne Helburn, Regina Greenspun, and Nathaniel Greenspun. In thanking them, we do not want to imply that all of them agree with all of it. Our spouses, Fred Bergmann and Julia Bush, gave many valuable suggestions and were supportive throughout. Last but not least, we thank Ellen McCarthy, our editor at the University of Michigan Press, for her faith in the project and her indispensable help in carrying it out.

Bill and Betty Boomer, like lots of other Americans, are worried about Social Security

Betty Boomer's parents, Ed and Ethel Elderly, 75, have also heard that the Social Security system is in trouble. The basic idea of Social Security is that, when you retire, you get a pension that the government will pay as long as you live. When people feel they can rely on Social Security, they are relieved of the worry that they will end their days in destitution or be dependent on their children. But the predictions of Social Security's bankruptcy have robbed many people of their peace of mind.

Social Security has two other kinds of benefits, besides pensions, that insure Americans against extreme hardship. If a worker dies leaving a child, Social Security will pay survivors' benefits to the family. If a worker becomes disabled before the age of retirement and can't work, Social Security will provide disability benefits. Of the 44 million people receiving benefits, 30 million are retirees and their dependents, 6 million are disabled workers and their dependents, and 7 million are survivors of deceased workers.

Retired people are worried too

The Boomers' daughter and son-in-law, Sue and Steve Sprout, are in their twenties and won't retire until well into the twenty-first century. They have heard many times that Social Security will be nonexistent by the time they retire. That makes them edgy about paying into the Social Security system and more willing to listen to suggestions that the system we have should be abandoned.

Many young people doubt they will ever benefit from Social Security

Everybody has heard claims that Social Security has no future, and many people have come to believe it. You almost never hear it said that Social Security's problems are fixable and that there is plenty of time to do the fixing.

Pollsters' Question: How confident are you, yourself, in the future of the Social Security System?

	Answers Given In:	
	1976	1998
Very confident	18%	7%
Somewhat confident	39	28
Not too confident	32	33
Not at all confident	10	26
Don't know	1	6

Scary predictions often get on TV and into the press

People need straight and clear answers about what Social Security's problems are and how they can be fixed. It helps if they know how the system works. Fortunately, it isn't hard to understand.

But are these stories about Social Security really true?

Social Security can't go bankrupt. A business can go bankrupt when it needs to make payments but doesn't have enough money to make them and has no place to get the money it needs. The same is true for a person. But Social Security can never be in that fix.

Social Security gets the money it needs to make benefit payments from taxes. Those taxes can be adjusted, when necessary, by our democratic processes. Social Security payments can be adjusted in the same way.

Could the Social Security system go bankrupt, leaving the old people without support?

The money to pay the Social Security benefits that retired people get in any year comes from the Social Security taxes that are collected that same year from people still working.

The Social Security system is run on a "pay as you go" plan in which each generation of workers pays for the pensions of their retired parents and grandparents. In other words, the retired don't get their benefits out of a pot of dollars they have personally put into the Social Security system. Those dollars have already been used to pay for the pensions of the generation that retired ahead of them. When you retire, the money to pay your pension will come from the taxes of the younger people still working.

So when Betty Boomer says, "We've been paying into Social Security for a long time. Where did all the money go?" the answer is, "To pay for the pensions of your own mom and dad."

The Social Security system was designed to have total taxes about equal to total benefits each year. If, in any year, the taxes paid to Social Security are bigger than the benefits that are scheduled to be paid, then the extra money is sent to the U.S. Treasury in exchange for U.S. Government Bonds. The collection of those bonds in the hands of the Social Security agency is called the "Social Security Trust Fund."

The bonds have never yet been used to pay Social Security benefits. Instead, benefits are paid directly out of the taxes collected. In the future bonds in the Trust Fund could be cashed to get money that could be used to pay part of the benefits. But the main source of Social Security benefits in any year will always be the taxes collected that year.

The benefits being paid today come out of the taxes being paid today

The current Social Security taxes will pay for the current Social Security benefits (with some help from the Trust Fund) at least until the year 2036, a third of a century into the future. Most economists think we could go without changing tax rates and benefit formulas considerably longer. But we can look ahead and see that at some time in the future taxes and benefits will get out of balance and adjustments will be needed.

Some critics of the system call the Social Security system "actuarially unsound" because it isn't set to run forever on automatic pilot without adjusting taxes and benefits. But Social Security is a program for the benefit of the whole nation, and the nation can be called upon to accept changes in taxes and benefits when they are needed. The amounts to be paid out in Social Security benefits and collected from Social Security taxes depend on how fast the number of workers in our nation grows, on how many retired people there are, on life expectancy, and on how the nation's economy develops. All of these change as time goes by, and adjustments have to be made when such changes push Social Security taxes and benefits out of balance.

The fact that such adjustments need to be made from time to time does not mean the program is unsound or dishonest or unstable. In fact, the ability of the government to make these adjustments is one of the great strengths of the system and will allow Social Security to continue as long as the American people want it to.

If we keep the taxes and the benefits in balance (and we can) there can't be any problem

The amounts of Social Security benefits and the taxes that pay for them have been set by Act of Congress.

To be eligible for a Social Security pension, you have to pay Social Security taxes for at least 40 quarter-years. A lesser-earning spouse, usually the wife, gets a benefit equal to 50 percent of the husband's benefit or a benefit based on her own earnings, whichever is higher. When one spouse dies, the surviving spouse receives a benefit equal to the husband's benefit or the wife's benefit, whichever is larger.

The current formula gives people retiring at age 65 who had average earnings a benefit that replaces 42 percent of their earnings. Those whose earnings were half the average get 53 percent of their earnings replaced. Those whose earnings were twice the average get a replacement of 28 percent of their earnings.

This means:

1. Social Security benefits are not at all lavish. Retired people are not living high on the hog, nor are they more comfortable than people who are still working.
2. Lower-wage workers get a higher percentage of their wages replaced when they retire than higher-wage workers. So the program causes some redistribution of income.

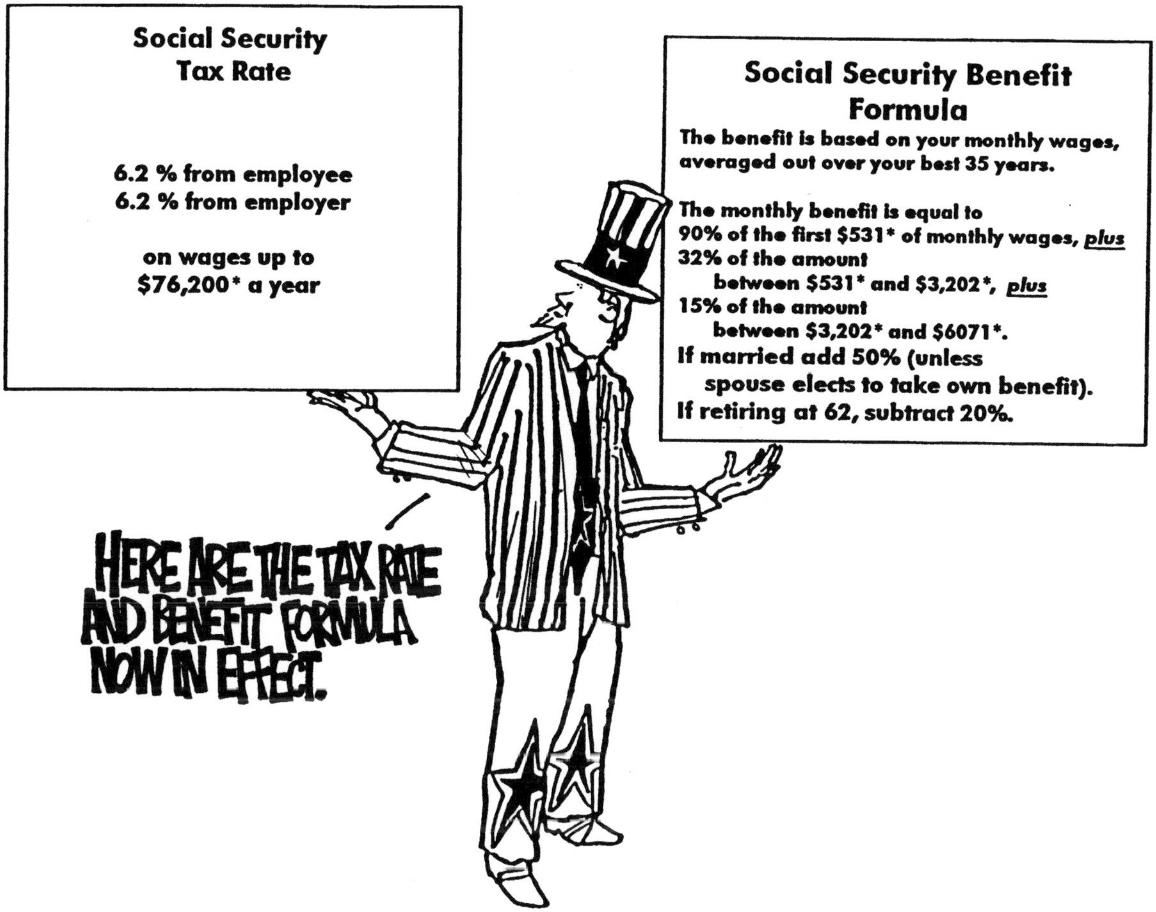

* These values apply in the year 2000.
They are adjusted yearly as average wages rise.

Today's taxes and benefits were set by Congress

In the past Congress has changed Social Security taxes and benefits whenever adjustments were needed or desired.

Social Security taxes are changed by amendments to the Federal Insurance Contributions Act, so the tax is sometimes called "the FICA."

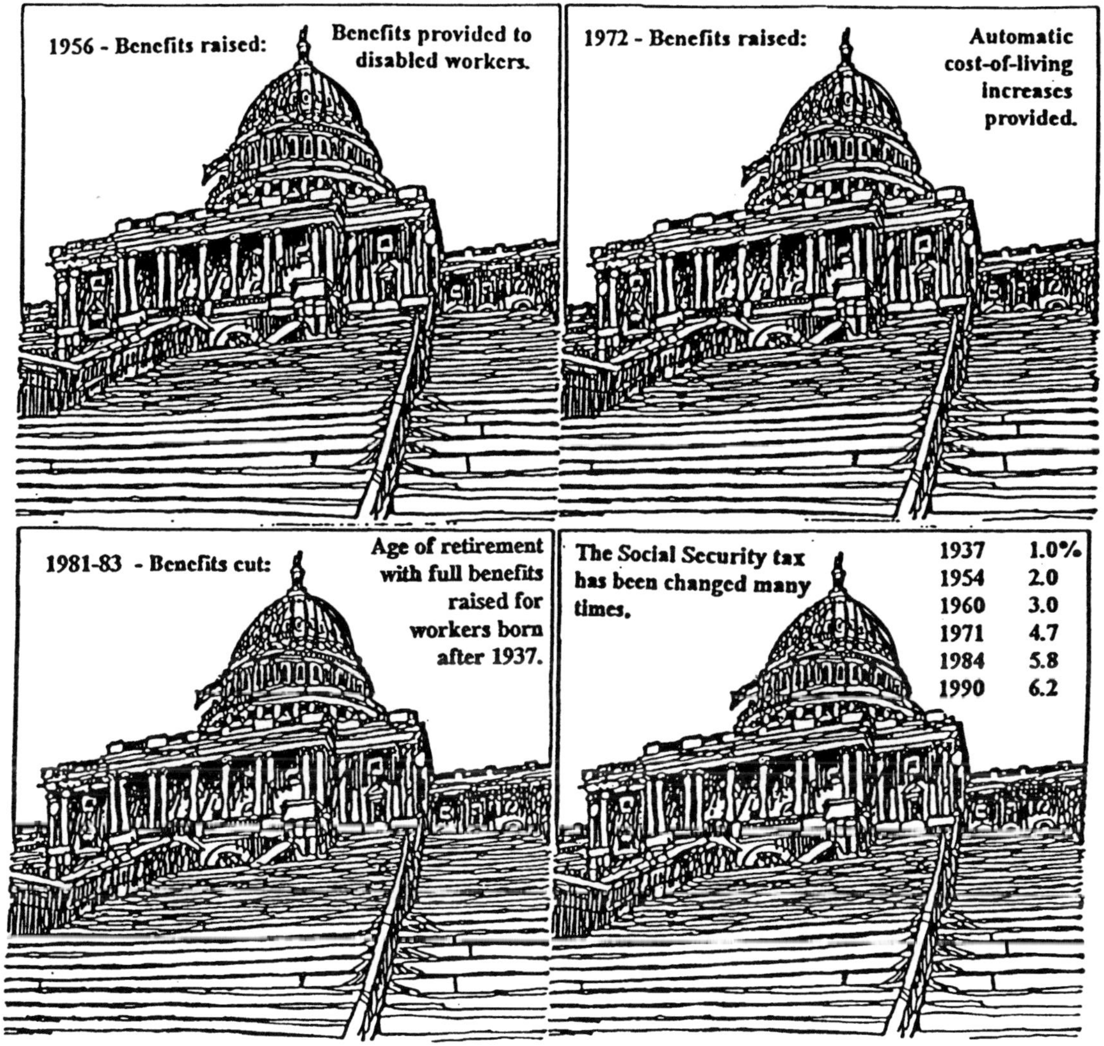

If taxes and benefits get out of balance Congress will adjust them, as it has done in the past

Currently, the Social Security tax rate that Congress has set produces more than enough money to pay the pensions for the Elderly generation. The big Boomer generation is still working, and their Social Security taxes help pay for the Elderlys' benefits.

There is no problem right now: The Baby Boomers are still working and paying taxes

The wave of Boomer retirements will start in 2008, and as they retire they will stop paying Social Security taxes and start collecting benefits. Even so, the money coming into Social Security will be enough to pay the currently scheduled benefits until about 2022. For a while after that, the Social Security agency can supplement the tax money it gets by cashing the bonds in the Trust Fund. In about 2036, the Trust Fund would run out of bonds. Only after that would some legal changes be needed in taxes or benefits.

But when the Boomers retire, Social Security will need to send out many more benefit checks

Life expectancy has been increasing and that will increase the number of Social Security benefit checks that need to go out as time goes on. A person who retired at age 65 in 1940 could expect to spend about 13 years in retirement. A person retiring at age 65 in the year 2000 can expect to spend about 18 years in retirement, which is 40 percent longer. Actuaries estimate that by the year 2050 another two years will have been added.

Year a Person Retires at Age 65	Average Number of Years Spent in Retirement
1940	12.71
1960	14.52
1980	16.33
1990	17.09
2000	17.83
2010	18.25
2020	18.68
2030	19.10
2040	19.51
2050	19.90
2060	20.29

The large size of the Boomer generation is a temporary burden on the Social Security system, although one that will last for decades. The burden due to the increase in life expectancy is permanent and growing. It has inspired calls to increase the standard age of retirement, the age at which a person can retire with full benefits.

The Boomers aren't the only problem—people are living longer

To keep the Social Security system going as the Boomers retire and to cover increases in life expectancy, we could simply raise taxes. Or we could cut benefits. Or we could do some of each. None of these changes would be very welcome, but some change is unavoidable. There is no magically painless way to get rid of the extra burden that the Boomers' retirement will cause. That burden will be put on the Sprouts, the generation following the Boomers, as well as on still younger workers.

While the Sprouts and their fellow workers will have to carry the extra burden of the Boomers' retirement, the burden of the Sprouts' own retirement should not be as tough for the generations that come after them, since there are fewer of them. So unless the Social Security system is dismantled, the Sprouts' worries about getting Social Security pensions is baseless.

When the Boomers retire, how will we get taxes and benefits back in balance?

When the Boomers retire, we can keep the present benefit formula as is and solve the problem simply by raising Social Security taxes. How high would those taxes have to go?

What if we just raised taxes and didn't touch benefits?

The problem of the Boomers would be solved if the Social Security tax on both workers and employers were raised from 6.2 percent to 7.8 percent—not now but around the year 2036. If we did that, no changes in benefits would be required.

All Social Security benefits are paid now out of money collected by a tax on wages. But we could get some of the additional tax money in other ways. We could use money raised by the income tax or a sales tax to pay for some of those benefits.

Such a rise in taxes would represent a 26 percent increase in the amount of money devoted to pensions. The Boomers' medical care bills would also be big, and additional money would have to be devoted to covering them, through Medicare. So, covering the Boomers' costs entirely by tax hikes would end up increasing the proportion of government spending devoted to supporting the aged considerably.

Doing the whole job with tax increases is
possible, but we have other options

We could make the tax increases smaller or do without them entirely if we cut some benefits to retirees. As we might expect, each possible cut in benefits has disadvantages.

Possible benefit cut #1: Give reduced benefits to the well-off. We could cut the benefits of seniors who have lots of income from other sources. If we cut Social Security benefits by 30 percent for people with retirement incomes over $60,000 and by 85 percent for those with incomes over $110,000, that would eliminate three-quarters of the problem.

Making benefits depend on other income would complicate the administration of the program, which now runs smoothly. It would probably weaken support for Social Security among the better-off people, who are the ones with the most influence and most likely to vote. It is also claimed that Social Security might come to be stigmatized as "welfare," a charity given to (rather than earned by) the weaker members of our society, and therefore something people should be ashamed of taking, rather than something they receive proudly, as they do now. Any stigma is unlikely, however, since the vast majority of retirees have incomes of less than $60,000.

We could cut benefits going to the rich

Possible benefit cut #2: Cut the "spouse benefit." At present a married person who is retired gets benefits that are 50 percent higher than a single person, provided the spouse doesn't claim a Social Security benefit based on his or her own work record. That extra boost is a relic from the time when most wives didn't work and were entitled to minimal or no benefits of their own. Suggestions have been made to cut the "spouse benefit" to 33 or 25 percent.

In many cases the spouse benefits result in larger pensions for one-earner couples than for two-earner couples with the same total income. So, the spouse benefits might be considered unfair to many married couples as well as to single people.

Or we could cut the big bonus that retired married couples get

Possible benefit cut #3: Tax Social Security benefits as we do private pensions. Social Security benefits are taxed much more lightly than private pensions. If we ended that special treatment for Social Security benefits, the extra tax money could come back to the Social Security system and help pay for benefits.

A worker's own contributions to a private pension fund (on which income tax has already been paid) is exempt from further tax. The rest of private pension income is fully taxable. Retired married couples over 65 were liable to tax on their private pensions if their income in 1998, including the taxable portion of those pensions, was greater than $15,900.

By contrast, no portion of Social Security benefits is currently taxable to a couple unless half of their Social Security benefits plus their other income comes to more than $32,000.

The exemption from taxation of most Social Security benefits probably derives from the feeling that the government should not be giving benefits with one hand and taxing them away with the other. But given the need to make adjustments that will balance out Social Security tax revenues and benefits, that argument may be less persuasive than it has been in the past. This change would erase 21 percent of the projected gap between Social Security revenues and benefits.

We tax Social Security benefits very lightly; we could tax them more

Possible benefit cut #4: Raise the age at which a person can retire with full benefits. Congress has already voted that the standard age of retirement, the age at which one gets full benefits, should be raised gradually from 65 to 67. We could make that standard age of retirement even higher.

There are good arguments against doing that. Currently, people can choose to retire at age 62, but they get 20 percent less in benefits if they do. As the standard age of retirement is increased, those retiring at 62 will have to take still bigger benefit cuts.

Some of the people retiring before the standard age of retirement have lost their jobs and despair of finding another because of age discrimination. Others have jobs that are physically demanding, and they have trouble doing the work. It would be cruel to reduce still further the standard of living of people who, for such reasons, retire early.

We could raise the standard age of retirement—but should we?

Raising the retirement age would be a severe hardship for workers who have developed arthritis by their early sixties, who have back trouble, or have developed other physical conditions that make work especially difficult. It would also be hard on people in boring jobs.

People are not only living longer but on average are healthier at higher ages than they used to be. Yet not everybody is so lucky. There are many people in their early sixties for whom retirement is a much-needed relief.

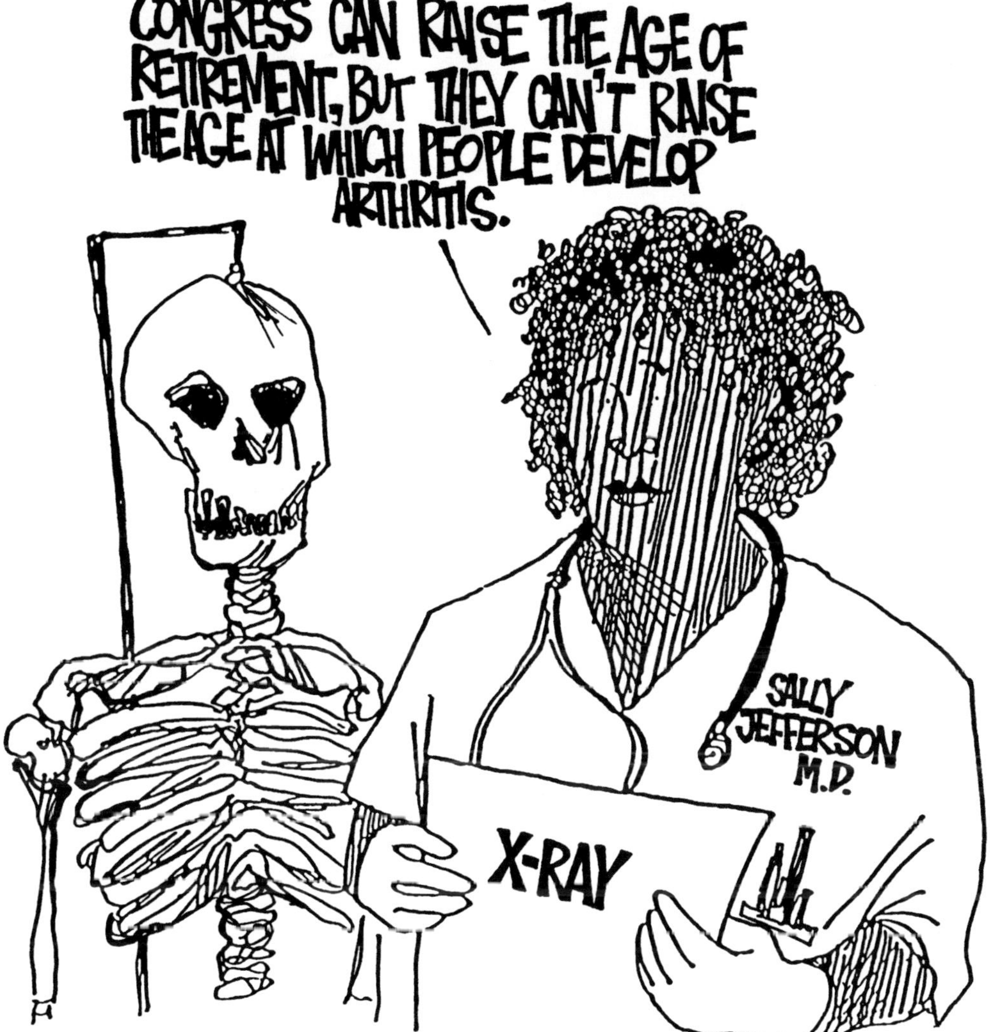

For some people, working past sixty-five
would be a terrific hardship

Last, but not least, here is one of the best ideas for raising money for Social Security. As of now, any wage income over $76,200 is exempt from Social Security taxes. We could repeal that "cap" on taxable wages. We could also make people contribute to Social Security out of the income they get from interest, dividends, and capital gains.

Removing the cap on the wages subject to the Social Security tax would bring in money that could pay for Social Security benefits, but it would also make the tax more fair. People with low or middling wages pay a Social Security tax on every dollar of wage income, while some of the wage income earned by the affluent escapes any Social Security tax. For this reason the Social Security tax is "regressive"—it is harder on the poor than on the rich.

There has always been a cap on benefits, and the original designers of the system put into the rules a corresponding cap on the wages subject to Social Security tax. In the past, whenever the cap on taxable wages has been pushed up, the cap on benefits has also been raised. This has meant that, as more money comes into the system as taxes, more is spent as benefits. But we do not have to retain this feature of the original system. We can keep the cap on benefits without exempting any wage income (or perhaps any other kind of income) from taxation for Social Security. The tax that supports Medicare has no cap; it covers all wage income, even though upper-income taxpayers don't get any more benefits than the rest of the population.

Earnings over $76,200 are now free of Social Security tax; taxing them would bring in money, make things fairer

A few of these adjustments in taxes and benefits will take care of the problem of the Boomers' retirement. We wouldn't need all of them.

But, if Social Security's future problems can be fixed fairly easily, why do so many people say the system is on its last legs and that the Sprouts will never get any benefits?

The politicians have not been interested in informing the American people that the Social Security system can be very easily shored up and that there is no danger that it will stop paying pensions. Those politicians who want to tear down the system want the public to think that bankruptcy looms. Some of those who might favor keeping the present system intact want credit for "saving Social Security."

The rumors about the death of the Social Security system are meant to frighten us into doing major surgery on a system that doesn't need it. Who is trying to frighten us? The next few pages tell the story.

So what's all the scare talk about?

All this "bankruptcy" talk originates with people who don't want to repair the Social Security system. They want to destroy it and replace it with a "private" system. Privatization would replace Social Security, a system in which the government promises workers they will get a pension when they retire, with a system in which each worker has a private account at a brokerage house, a bank, or an insurance company. Workers would pay money into their accounts instead of paying Social Security taxes, and their retirement income would come out of those accounts.

Those in favor of privatization differ in how much freedom they think the owners of the private accounts should have. Some privatizers would allow total freedom, both to pick investments and to decide when and how much money to withdraw from the account after retirement. Others would allow only certain investments and would require the purchase of annuities with the money in the accounts. (When you buy an annuity, you get a contract with an insurance company that promises to pay you a fixed monthly cash payment for as long as you live.)

If there were maximum freedom, we could expect to see large numbers of penniless old people.

There are those who don't want to fix
Social Security—they want to kill it

The main advocates of privatization are Wall Street firms and other companies in the financial services industry that look forward to making fat commissions—billions of dollars—if the money collected for Social Security were diverted to them.

Not everybody in the financial services industry favors privatization. Some worry that a privatization scheme might turn into a big fiasco, bringing with it millions of small accounts that would be costly to administer as well as more regulation, which might affect their regular business.

People on Wall Street want to earn fees
for managing private pension accounts

The brokers and financial services companies that want Social Security replaced by a private scheme have converted quite a few politicians to their point of view.

The financial services industry contributes more money to both Democratic and Republican politicians than any other industry does. So it is no wonder that there are politicians in both parties who support privatization.

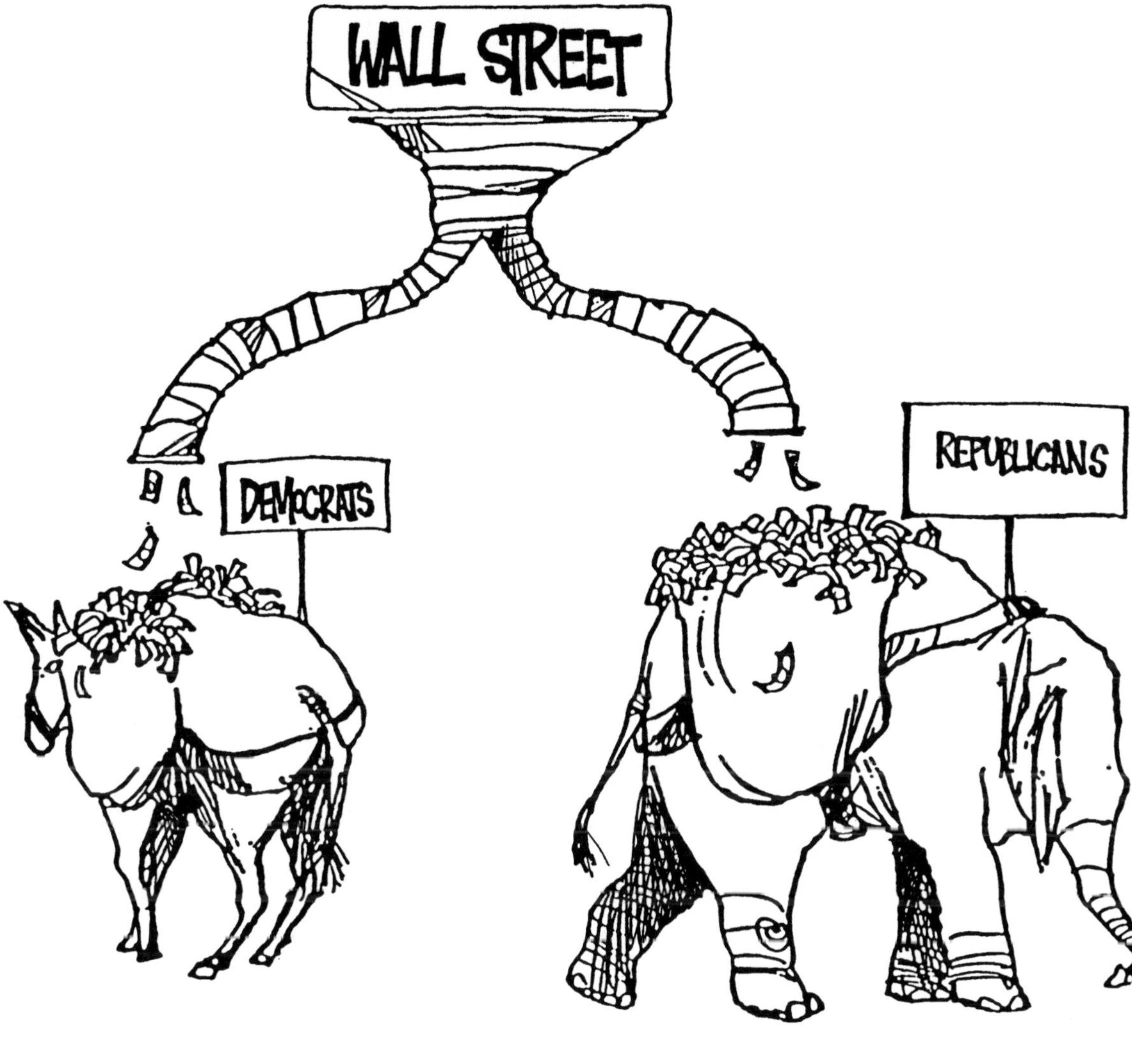

Many politicians have been converted: The financial industry has been showering them with money

Other enemies of our present Social Security system include the folks who hate the idea of the federal government and are against anything it does. Social Security is the largest program of the U.S. government, so they hate it.

People who despise the government despise Social Security

Some economists claim the American economy would grow faster if Social Security were converted into a private system. Others disagree.

The economists favoring privatization say it would lead to more saving, more investment, and therefore a bigger economy. A privatized system would be "prefunded"—people would get pensions from accounts that had been accumulated ahead of time, rather than relying for their pensions on the taxes paid by younger citizens in the same year. Creating these accounts, these economists claim, would raise the level of saving in the country.

This argument might or might not work out in practice. More saving, assuming it occurs, doesn't always lead to more productive capacity for the economy. People save by reducing what they spend for their living expenses, which can lead to unemployment and recession, unless businesses increase investment to make up the difference.

Some economists think (and others do not) that privatizing
Social Security would improve the economy

In a fully privatized pension system the money in a private account could be invested as the worker wishes. The amount of retirement income would depend on how well the investments work out.

In a privatized system people could choose their own investments

Those who want to privatize the system claim that private accounts would produce a lot more money for retirees, giving them a better return on their contributions than the Social Security system does.

The advocates of privatization sometimes imply that under their system anybody (perhaps everybody) could accumulate substantial fortunes by being allowed to invest for themselves the money they would have paid in Social Security taxes. Could every old person be rich and lead the life of a wealthy person in retirement? Could we all end up as aged millionaires? The answer is *no, not really.*

It has been claimed that if we privatized retired people would receive three times what they would get under the current Social Security benefits formula. Either total real income in the country would have to rise as a result of privatization enough to pay the larger pensions–about 20 percent—or the extra purchasing power for the retired population would come out of the hides of younger people who are still working. But there is no indication that privatizing the Social Security system would increase total real income by 20 percent.

Something that sounds too good to be true usually *is* too good to be true.

Some private investments might do really well.
Why not give people that opportunity?

Replacing Social Security with private accounts would create big problems.

Privatization problem #1: Stocks can go down as well as up. The Japanese stock market, for example, started to slide downward in 1989. By 1998, the average stock had lost two-thirds of its value. It could happen here. If your pension were based on the value of stocks, and you happened to retire in a period in which stock prices were severely depressed, your pension could be severely reduced.

Privatization can produce big problems:
Problem #1: Stocks can fall disastrously

Privatization problem #2: Social Security benefits keep up with inflation. Every year benefits are raised by the same percentage as prices have increased, preserving the purchasing power of the pension intact. No private investments could guarantee that.

If you had retired in 1985 with a pension that was *not* protected against inflation, by the year 2000 the purchasing power of your pension would have eroded by 38 percent. You might have fallen below the poverty line and be in big trouble.

Privatization problem #2: Private pensions lack protection from inflation

Privatization problem #3: Some Americans would pick some very wrong things to invest in. Some would invest in legitimate businesses that failed; others would become the victims of outright fraud. When these people got old, they'd be in terrible shape financially. The Social Security system now protects people from making mistakes like that. With privatization they would lose that protection.

Some of the penniless oldsters could get help from their own sons and daughters. Others would have no place to turn to but the government, which could perhaps give them welfare payments. Of course, the country might decide to let them suffer without help as an example to others of what not to do.

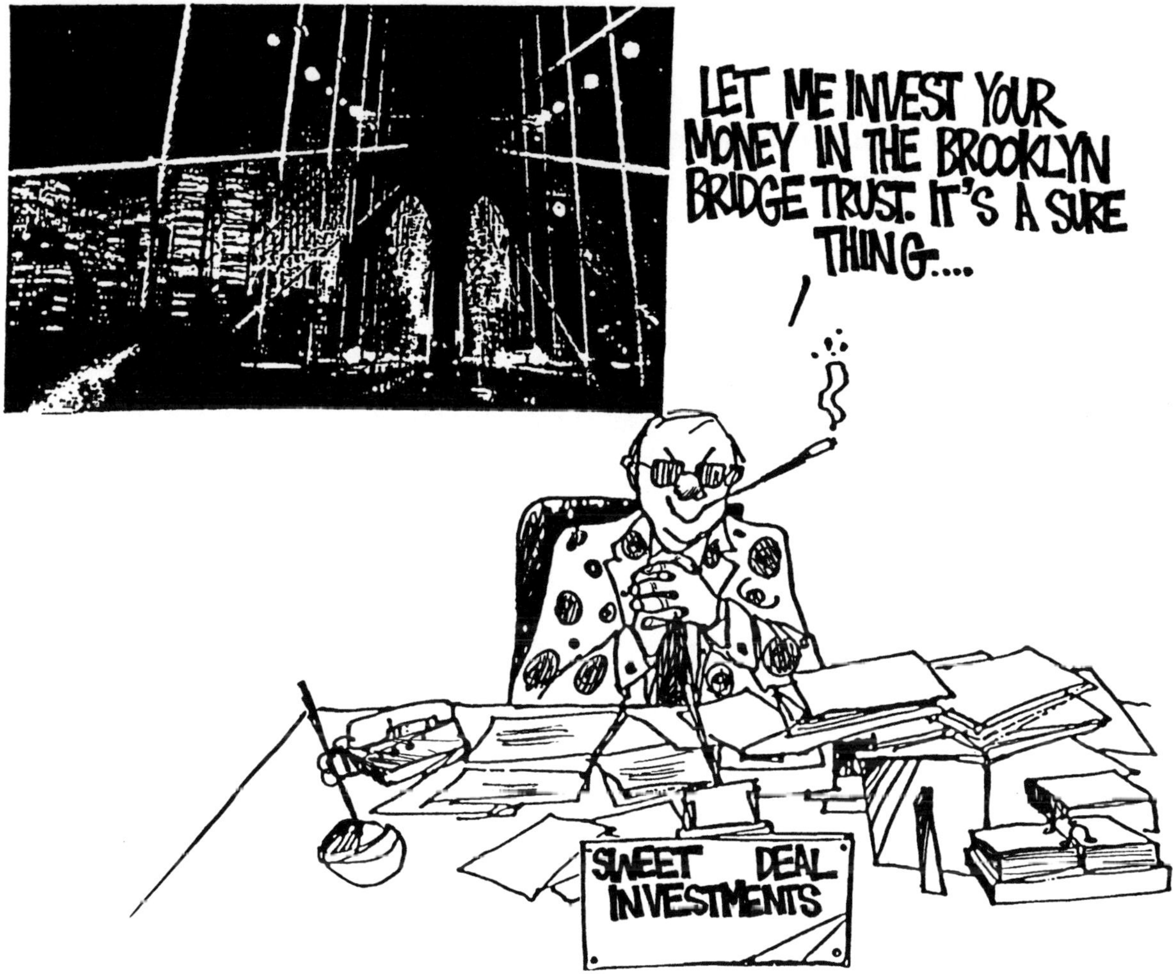

Privatization problem #3: Not everybody would avoid investment pitfalls

Privatization problem #4: The investment of the private accounts could be controlled by the government, which would reduce the risk of bad investment choices by individual citizens. But then the federal government would be a major investor in American companies and would have a great incentive to boss them around.

The current chairman of the Federal Reserve System, Alan Greenspan, is among those who think that government-controlled investments in the stock market are likely to trigger government interference in the operations of private business. Others believe that there are ways to insulate business from the government's involvement.

Privatization problem #4: Government investment might bring interference

Privatization problem #5: A lot of money would go into brokerage fees and other costs of administering the private accounts.

Some other countries (England and Chile, for example) have privatized their Social Security systems. In those countries about 20 percent of the benefits money is being skimmed off by private financial institutions for administration fees. Our Social Security Administration spends less than 1 percent of its budget on administration.

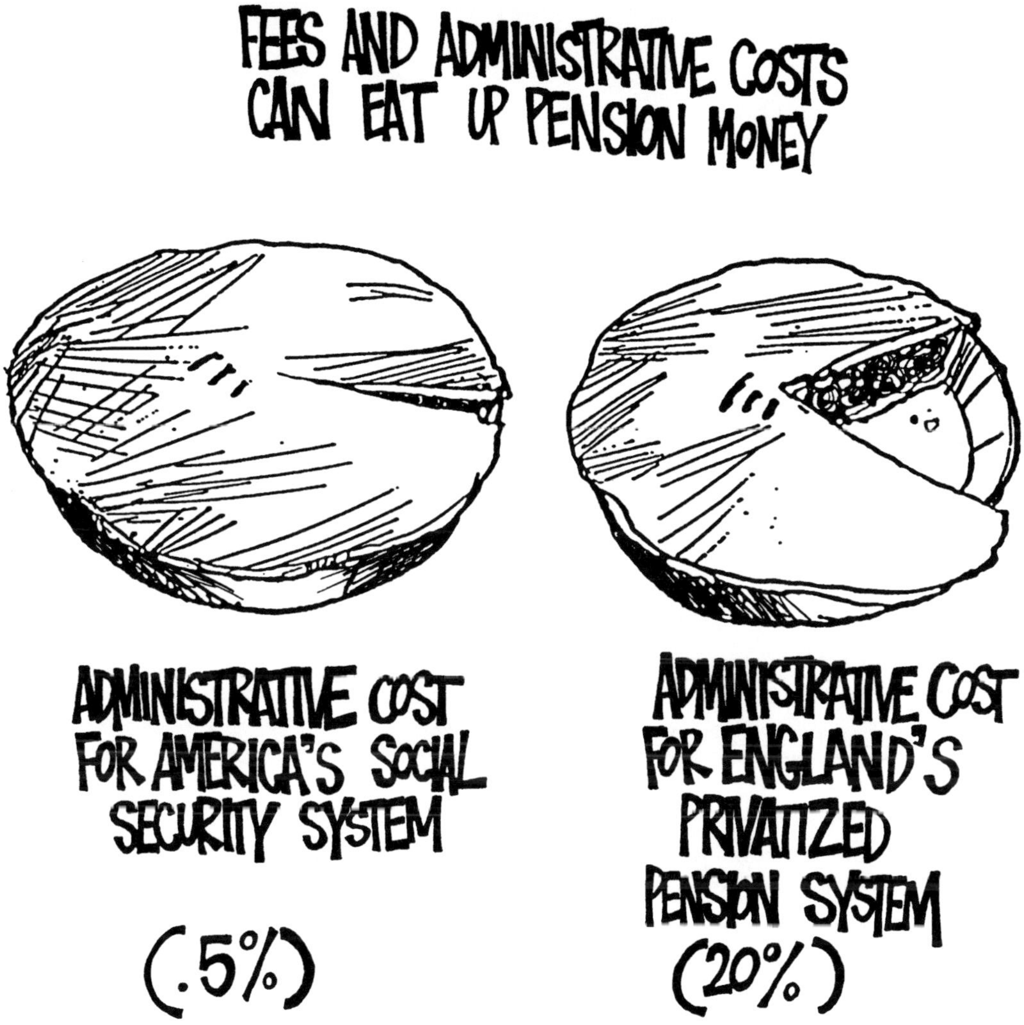

Privatization problem #5: A private system can drain off money for big fees

Privatization problem #6: The Sprouts, the generation following the Boomers, would have to bear a double burden with privatization.

1. Paying Social Security taxes to finance the Boomers' retirement. (The Boomers wouldn't have private accounts to get their pensions from.)
2. Paying extra taxes for the money going into the Sprouts' own private accounts.

The Sprouts, unlike any other generation so far, would have to pay for its own pensions *and* pay for the pensions of its parents' and grandparents' generation as well. If we stay with the present system and avoid privatization, the Sprouts will have more of a load financing the pension system than other generations have had because of the size of the Boomers' generation. They don't need yet an additional burden paying the costs of the transition to a privatized system.

Some of the privatizers recognize that the terrible burden the Sprouts would have to bear is a problem. They suggest that the government should borrow $1,900,000,000,000 (that's almost two trillion dollars). This money would pay regular Social Security pensions to the retired Boomers, and the Sprouts' Social Security taxes could go into private accounts instead of into the Boomers' pensions, spreading these "transition costs" to the generations that come after the Sprouts. It would probably also soak up any extra savings that the transition to privately funded pensions was intended to generate. Extra savings is touted as the virtue of a privatized system, and this proposal for big borrowing undermines that argument.

Of course, we could avoid these huge transition costs by just sticking to the present Social Security system.

Privatization problem #6: Young workers would have a double burden

Privatization problem #7: Putting Social Security money into the stock market and later taking it out to pay pensions might make the ups and downs of the stock market more extreme.

In a privatized system retired people whose pensions are entirely dependent on the stock market might have big fluctuations in their standard of living. If the investment in the stock market were made by the government, then it might be politically impossible for the government to sell stocks during periods when the market was falling.

Privatization problem #7: Huge Social Security funds moving in and out of the market could destabilize it

President Clinton has offered a plan to "save Social Security"—using the budget surplus to pay off most of the national debt. This move would not, in any direct way, clear up the problems caused by the size of the Boomer generation and greater life expectancy. Moreover, paying off the national debt might create some further problems, such as a serious recession.

Paying off the debt would reduce the amount of federal tax money that would have to be used to pay interest to bondholders in the future, making it somewhat easier to shovel tax money into the Social Security system when the Boomers retire. It would also have the effect of lowering interest rates, which is sometimes good for economic growth.

Money is available to the government for paying off the debt when it has a surplus—when it takes more money out of the economy by taxation than it uses for spending on government programs. It uses the extra tax money to buy government bonds from the public. This has the effect of depressing the demand for goods and services and reducing the number of jobs. When the economy is too hot, it is appropriate to reduce the debt; when the economy is sluggish and unemployment is too high, it is appropriate to run a deficit. Which is appropriate at any time depends on how the economy is doing. A rigid plan to run a surplus for many years, regardless of the condition of the economy, could be destructive to our prosperity. It could cause the surplus itself to disappear, as lower employment cuts tax revenue.

Other uses for the surplus: programs to help with our urgent national needs, such as child care, better schools, and health insurance for all. Tax cuts are another possible use.

A nonsolution that might do harm: Paying off the national debt

If we decide against privatization and in favor of getting Social Security into balance by some combination of benefit cuts and tax increases, when is the right time to do it?

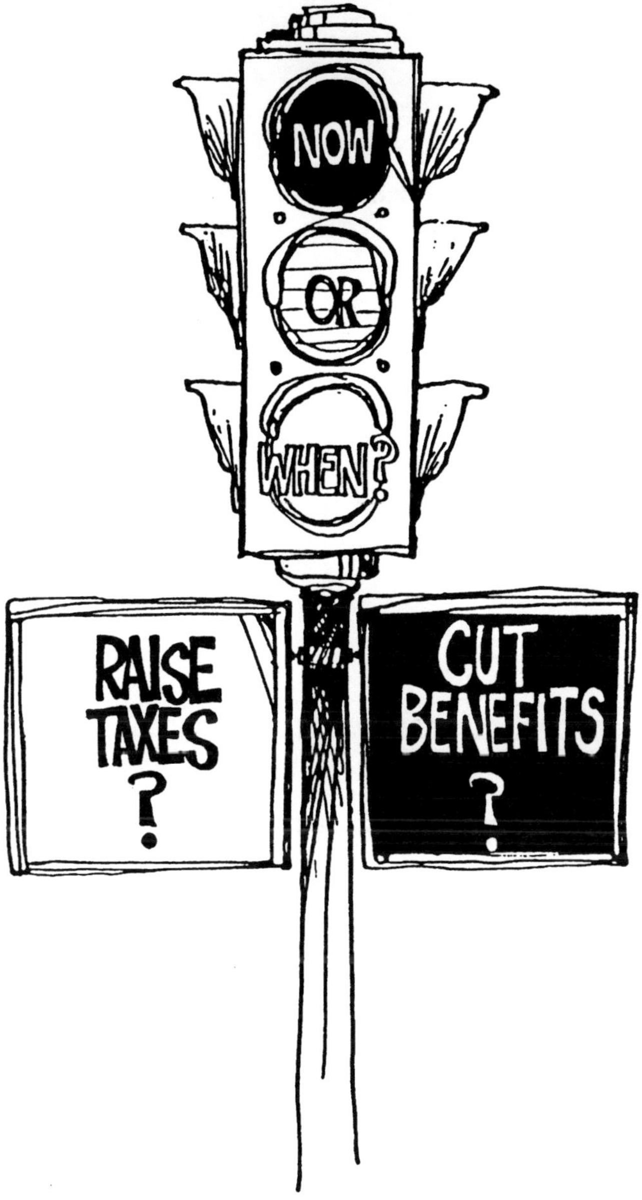

When should we fix Social Security?

A lot of people are saying we need to start saving Social Security right now.

Is now the time?

If we are planning to cut benefits in the future and increase the retirement age, we should give plenty of advance notice so that people can plan for it.

People need advance notice of changes in benefits

We shouldn't increase Social Security taxes ahead of the time we will need the extra money for pensions. Doing that would not make it easier to pay for pensions in the future. As we have seen, when the Social Security agency has had extra money, it has sent it to the Treasury, which has used it to pay for regular federal government expenditures, such as buying fighter planes. When that happens, the Treasury prints up bonds and sends them to the Social Security Administration in return, which it keeps in a drawer marked "Social Security Trust Fund."

The bonds in the Trust Fund represent a formal promise that the Treasury will send a certain amount of money to the Social Security agency when Social Security taxes don't cover benefits. But does such a promise really add anything to the security of our older people? That security rests not on some printed papers in a drawer, but on the will of the American people to see that our elders are not destitute. When the Treasury is asked to redeem the bonds in the Trust Fund with money that could be used to pay for pensions, it will have to sell bonds to the public or send the Social Security system money from the income tax or the corporation tax. But this could be done whether there are bonds in the Trust Fund drawer or not. So raising the Social Security tax prematurely and adding to the pieces of paper in the Trust Fund drawer doesn't add anything to the security of the Boomers' pensions, and doesn't increase the real resources available to pay for those pensions.

Raising Social Security taxes ahead of need is a bad move—the extra money goes to other uses

When the Boomers retire, all we will have to show for the Social Security tax money the Treasury sent to the Pentagon will be a bunch of old warplanes. Those planes are not going to help us support the elderly.

Politicians who want to reduce government spending have criticized using that part of the Social Security tax money that is not needed to pay benefits on other government programs. They say this amounts to "looting Social Security." But, when Social Security taxes are raised prematurely, sending the extra money to the Treasury to be spent on things the country needs (not necessarily defense spending) is most often the best way to use it. Unless the economy is overheating, the extra money is best put back into circulation through government purchases. Otherwise, it becomes a drag on the economy and increases unemployment.

The best plan would be to keep transfers to the other government programs low by keeping Social Security taxes and benefits in balance and providing for other government programs with the income tax and the corporation tax.

The extra Social Security taxes buy things that can't be used by the retired

The Social Security tax falls most heavily on low-income workers, so we should keep it as low as possible, just high enough to finance current pensions. (Some people go further and think we should finance Social Security pensions mostly or entirely with the income tax.) A big premature raise in the Social Security tax took place during the Reagan administration, and personal income taxes and corporate taxes, which fall more heavily on the well-to-do, were decreased. As a result, 15 percent of regular government spending, which used to be financed mostly by income and corporate taxes, is now being financed by money from the regressive Social Security tax. Raising the Social Security tax again before we need the revenue for the Boomers' pensions would worsen the situation. It's just a sneaky way of relieving the well-off of a substantial part of the burden of supporting regular government expenditure.

Social Security taxes shouldn't be raised and benefits shouldn't be lowered until we need to do it.

We need to keep a good balance between taxes and benefits

People have argued that Social Security is a flawed system that needs changing, but there is an answer to each of their objections.

Objection #1: Social Security is a terrible investment. People could do better investing their own money.

Answer: Social Security isn't an investment. It's a system in which each generation supports its parents and grandparents.

Is Social Security a bad investment? No, it's each generation giving support to its elders

Objection #2: We need to change the system so as to escape the burden of the Boomers' retirement costs.

Answer: There is really no way for the Sprout generation to escape the burden of supporting the retired Boomers.

The bread the Boomers will eat when they retire will have to be baked the day they eat it. The people of the Sprout generation, and those still younger who will be working and producing in those years will have to share the bread they bake (and the other products they produce) with the Boomers. That is the real burden the Boomers will create. There is no escaping it, whatever the changes we make in the arrangements for the financing of Americans' retirement income. Privatization would increase the burden that the Sprouts would have to carry, instead of relieving it.

The Boomers' retirement and longer lifespans will create burdens—there is no way to escape it

Objection #3: Social Security is unsound. We can look ahead and see there will come a time when the taxes won't finance the benefits.

Answer: Social Security is not a private insurance company that can go bankrupt. As long as the American people want to keep it going, we can. We can change the taxes and benefits when we need to.

But the American people have always been willing
to act responsibly toward their elders

Since the start of Social Security in President Roosevelt's administration, Americans have always chosen to shore it up when necessary to preserve a good level of benefits. Working Americans don't want their parents and grandparents to be forced to move in with them in order to survive.

The alternative to government-guaranteed pensions is not attractive

Even if the American economy grows more slowly than expected—at the modest rate of 1.2 percent per year—the per capita income of Americans by the year 2040 will be 65 percent higher than it is now. Just about one-third of that increase in income will pay for the increased costs of Social Security and Medicare. The rest will provide a big improvement in the standard of living. So we will certainly continue to be able to afford to provide benefits for our older citizens.

Destroying Social Security to "save it" is a terrible idea. It's a system that has served us well and can do so in the future.

Social Security can sail on smoothly, if we handle it right!

For Further Reading

Generally favorable to the present Social Security system

Dean Baker and Mark Weisbrot. *Social Security: The Phony Crisis.* Chicago: University of Chicago Press, 1999.

Henry J. Aaron and Robert D. Reischauer. *Countdown to Reform: The Great Social Security Debate.* New York: Century Foundation, 1998.

Max J. Skidmore. *Social Security and Its Enemies: The Case for America's Most Efficient Insurance Program.* Boulder, CO: Westview Press, 1999.

Steve Stecklow and Sara Callian. "Financial Flop: Social Security Switch in U.K. Is Disastrous: A Caution to the U.S.?" *Wall Street Journal,* August 10, 1998, A1.

In favor of privatization

Peter J. Ferrara and Michael D. Tanner. *Common Cents, Common Dreams: A Layman's Guide to Social Security Privatization.* Washington, DC: Cato Institute, 1998.

Laurence K. Kotlikoff and Jeffrey Sachs. "It's High Time to Privatize." *Brookings Review* (Summer 1997).

Carolyn L. Weaver. *The Frayed Social Contract; Why Social Security is in Trouble and How It Can Be Fixed.* Washington, DC: American Enterprise Institute, 2000.

World Bank. *Averting the Old Age Crisis: Policies to Protect the Old and Promote Growth.* New York: Oxford University Press, 1994.